Diary of a Mad Medium

*A Guide to Understanding
a Karmic Profile*

Diary of a Mad Medium

A Guide to Understanding a Karmic Profile

Melinda Vail

Dandelion Books, LLC
www.dandelion-books.com

Diary of a Mad Medium, by Melinda Vail
Hard Copy Version
ISBN 978-0-9992157-6-0
Library of Congress Catalog Card Number 2017957034

Front and back cover design by Jacqueline Summit, www.summitmarketingllc.com
Book layout and design by Accurance, www.accurance.com
A special thanks to Rees Candee for the front cover photo.

Disclaimer

Dandelion Books, LLC
Printed in the United States of America
www.dandelion-books.com

To James Van Praagh, the greatest spiritual teacher of all time...

An inspiration to all who teach after him.

Contents

Foreword

Melinda and I crossed paths many times over the years at various spiritual events, but it wasn't until 2016, at an event we hosted together in Scottsdale, Arizona, that I was exposed to her brilliant work on Karmic Profiling. That weekend I was blown away by Melinda's talent as a medium as well as her warmth and wisdom as a counselor, lecturer and spiritual coach.

At the start of our evening event, Melinda joined me on stage in a flowing white tunic. "Are you wearing a toga?" I jokingly asked her, but I could see that the woman I had known for over a decade was coming into her own in every way. I was delighted to see my friend so happy and glowing! The evening just got better and better, culminating with a reading in which Melinda brought through Pope John Paul II to his niece in the audience. As Melinda shared the deceased Pope's powerful message of love and tolerance, I could see jaws dropping around the room and I wondered, "How am I going to compete with this?!"

I shouldn't have worried. Melinda and I worked together to form a "double link" to Spirit, bringing through rich, detailed messages from the other side, and proving to all that the dead are always with us.

The next day at our full day Mediumship workshop, Melinda shared her insights about Karmic Profiling. I've always described this as the story of your Soul, which encompasses everything about its journey through many lifetimes. It includes Soul contracts and soul families;

understanding the lessons that your soul is sent to earth to learn; destiny; Karma; repeating patterns; addictions—all are part of the picture. But a concept this vast can be complicated to explain and difficult to understand.

I've never heard anyone paint such a clear picture of the Karmic Profile as Melinda did that day. She made this abstract topic real and relevant to everyone in the audience.

Diary of a Mad Medium, A Guide to Understanding a Karmic Profile is a gift to anyone who has ever asked themselves, "Who am I?", "Why am I here?", and "Why do I keep repeating the same old patterns?" The answers lie within these covers. Enjoy!

—James Van Praagh
Clairvoyant, Spiritual Medium, Author,
Producer, and Television Personality

Prologue

"All the world's a stage,
And all the men and women merely players;
They have their exits and their entrances;
And one man in his time plays many parts,
His acts being seven ages."

William Shakespeare

I want you to open up and expand your mind as you read about empowering yourself and learning how to love yourself. If you've read a lot of self-help books, been a good meditator, tried to follow what you've been taught about the "Law of Attraction" and you find that your patterns keep repeating themselves, then this book is for you.

Do you have repetitive patterns in your life? Are you seeing that your children are repeating patterns of your life or repeating patterns of your parents' lives? No matter what kind of therapy, visualizations or dream boards you've done, you just can't seem to stop repeating those patterns? Then it is time to start understanding your Karmic Profile.

FBI profilers figure out who the serial killer is by looking at aspects of the major personality and behavioral characteristics of an individual based upon analysis of the crime or crimes that person has committed. The challenge in your Karmic Profile is to find out who you really are at your core.

First, you have to recognize that your spirit lives in a "suitcase." The body is the container that the spirit chooses to be in on the "earth plane." Our job is to unpack the "suitcase" in order to be clear when we get to the other side. But more often than not, we are packing more into ourselves in a way that creates more Karma and we end up on the other side with a "heavier load."

It is because we haven't really been taught what our "purpose" is on the planet. We have many misunderstandings about that, which causes us to create more "baggage." We will talk about purpose in a later chapter in this book.

Second, you have to begin to understand that everything on this planet is about an energetic "transaction." It is the energy exchange between you and your parents, you and your relationships, you and your children, you and your co-workers, you and your friends, you and your acquaintances, you and strangers, and, most important, you with you.

In today's world with everything from Facebook to Instagram, our "energetic transactions" are coming back and forth at a fast and furious pace. It is a potent energy complication in an advanced world where we, as human souls, have to begin to recognize what we're doing energetically with our words and our deeds before it all comes crashing down.

We will discuss the five attributes to your current profile:

- Nature
- Nurture
- Akashic Records (the record of who you were in a past life and how much baggage you brought back and forth in your transactions, based on your transactional analysis for life review on the other side)
- Emotional and spiritual maturity
- Your understanding of God or the Universe

I always teach from my own Karmic Profile to make all of this clear. So, my name is Melinda but as a child I was known as Mindy. Mindy is my childhood nickname and I'll be talking about her as if she were separate from me, even though she is a part of me.

There are times that I choose to make her a part of me and other times when I choose to keep her separate because she represents the duality of who I am. That is another piece of what we must understand: the duality on this planet.

Duality in its simplest terms is the conflict between our ego and our spirit. In most major religions it is depicted as a devil and an angel, one riding on one shoulder, one on the other.

The reason there is duality on this planet is so we can learn to allow ourselves to move forward to a place where our spirit takes over and our ego is put in a neutral zone. Our spiritual goal is to get off of a planet of third dimension, get out of the cycle of reincarnation, and move to a different dimensional frequency.

Unfortunately, on this plant we suffer emotionally and physically. It is most important to recognize that all events on this planet are neutral, except for the emotion you assign to them. That said, you must figure out how you are assigning emotion. Sometimes your inner child or baggage from a past life will come out in ways you may not recognize. Your spirit, your subconscious mind, and your conscious mind are like a corporation in your body. Your spirit and your subconscious mind are "silent partners."

They are so silent, you don't even know they are there. But they are the moneymen; they hold the bottom line in the transaction. Unless you really dig and find out who you are from both subconscious and spiritual levels, you are never going to know who you *really* are and what your purposes are. All you will ever know is your ego.

The first step to understanding your current profile is to look at heredity. Right now, looking into ancestry is a "hot" thing to do. That's because our collective consciousness is beginning to understand we don't know who we are unless we know who our ancestors were. Many indigenous people have known that for a long time but many of us have forgotten. We have forgotten about our grandparents and our great-grandparents; however, it is beginning to reawaken within us right now. The first thing to do to understand your profile is to know your family background.

Act I

DNA: It's Already in There

Since I was raised in an Irish Catholic family, having intuition is part of a hereditary factor. The Irish are known to be a little superstitious as well as intuitive. In certain ways, superstition is a gateway to intuition. The ego uses the same gateway, however. Ireland is also a land of the ancient Celtic mystery, storytelling, fairies, and leprechauns. The Celtic people considered the trees to have knowledge. There are elves, gnomes, elementals, and banshees. In Irish mythology, a banshee is a female spirit or a fairy that heralds the death of a family member, usually by shrieking or keening (weeping or wailing).

This keening woman may in some cases be a professional, and the best keeners would be in high demand. As a medium and a person who helps families deal with a death, I suppose in certain ways I am the modern-day banshee. Although I don't believe in all the mythical information, I do affirm that it sets me up through my heritage to believe there is more to this world then what comes through my five senses.

Interestingly, one of the first movies produced by Walt Disney in 1959 was *Darby O'Gill and the Little People*, a movie about a wily Irishman battling wits with a leprechaun. On June 26, 1959, Darby O'Gill had its world premiere in Dublin, Ireland. June 26 was dubbed "Walt Disney Day" and a school holiday. All funds raised were given to St. Vincent de Paul for charity. The American premiere on June 26, 1959 took place in Grauman's Chinese theater in Hollywood, which was the first time a Disney release was featured there. So, obviously there is a little bit of ancient Celtic mysticism in all of us through our collective consciousness. After all, we do believe we are all a little bit Irish on Saint Paddy's Day here in the United States!

I believe my Catholicism also factored into my intuitive, psychic, and mediumship abilities. The Catholic Church teaches that it is the first Christian community established by Jesus Christ. It is the Church that Jesus Christ died for, and was built and established by the Apostles. Whether this supposition is true or not, let's just say it goes back a very long time. The first Church was established in 325 AD, during which Constantine, the Roman emperor from 306-337 AD, promoted the "Christianization" of pagan beliefs. This foundation allowed for ancient Irish pagan beliefs and some of the Catholic beliefs to become braided into my DNA.

When I was a child, this braiding manifested in my life. I went to grade school across the street from my Catholic Church. Every Tuesday afternoon with all the other Catholic children, we would leave school and walk across the street for our religious teachings. Both the Church and the school were within walking distance of my home. My mother told me that on the way home from school, I would lag behind the other children.

One day she decided she would walk down the street to find out what I was doing and why I would dawdle. She discovered that after school each day I would walk across the street and enter the Church. I remember I would kneel in a pew and then try to will the statues of Jesus and Mary to talk with me. I had watched a movie about the children of Fatima and would imagine myself to be in the movie.

I wanted to experience the Virgin Mother talking to me. I now know that I was meditating and training my brain to be able to speak to "the other side." I was teaching myself how to be a medium. Whether it came from a combination of the DNA and a past life, I do not know, but I believe both to be true. As a child, I would prefer a sign that my beliefs were true. Finally, a sign was revealed to me to me that cemented my faith.

In those days, women were not allowed up on the altar. One day when I was sitting in a pew alone, a priest came out on the altar and motioned for me to come up. He asked me to hold the chalice while he was cleaning. The chalice is considered a very sacred vessel to hold. To me this was a monumental sign that Jesus and Mary heard my prayers and that I was allowed to hold something that no young girl had ever been allowed to hold before.

The power of hope and faith are like the power of love, only tangible by experiencing them. And like love, the reasons for them can be a deeply personal riddle, perhaps unseen by others but very real to you. The existence of those feelings should never be questioned by another, as they are a part of one's own journey and of living within the ideals of integrity. We must allow each other the respect of what is real in another person's life.

That simple energetic transaction between this priest (whom I did not know) and me allowed my faith to deepen to the level that years later, as a medium I teach faith and life after life connection to thousands of people. One small act of kindness changed my life.

The resulting energy in my DNA is that at my basic core, I have a metaphysical belief system. Metaphysics can be defined as transcending physical matter within the laws of nature.

I took my daughter, Amanda, and grandson, Elliot (age 7), to Ireland for a visit. It was like going home for me. Everything about it resonated. It amazed me when talking to the Irish how the folklore has been kept alive. I have a very good friend, Pat McMahon, here in Phoenix, Arizona. Pat is a legend to our town. He starred in the children's show called *The Wallace and Ladmo Show* from 1954 to 1989. Pat played a variety of characters on this program and like Pat, the show itself has become somewhat of an urban legend. He also hosted a radio program called *The God Show,* where he interviewed people about religion and spirituality.

I met Pat when I appeared as a guest on his local TV talk show. After being asked back several times, he and his wife became good friends. My grandson Elliot calls him "Papa." On St. Patrick's Day, Papa Pat often plays a leprechaun and my grandson Elliot has seen him in costume.

One morning on our Irish trip, an Irish lad at the Dromoland Castle was giving us a tour. He was the archetypical young Irishman. He invited Elliot to sit up front with him in the horse-drawn carriage. He spoke with a thick Irish brogue and told us all about the superstitions and history of Dromoland Castle. He asked Elliott if he had ever seen a leprechaun. Elliot vehemently shook his head no. Then he proceeded to tell Elliot: "If you see a leprechaun, you got to grab him... you got to choke him... and you got to kill him! Because if you don't, you don't get the gold!"

Elliott turned to me wide-eyed and voicelessly mouthed "Papa Pat?" It was so funny.

In Their Own Words

Dear Melinda,

You are a true teacher and you possess a unique way of communicating the meanings of your messages. The class was very much appreciated and I know that everyone who attended received a healing simply by the energy felt in the room. This truly is your life's calling and I hope that many more people receive your messages as you help them realize what wonderful human beings they are.

—Francine

Act II

"Life's but a walking shadow,
A poor player that struts and frets
His hour upon the stage
And then is heard no more.
It is a tale told by an idiot,
Full of sound and fury,
Signifying nothing."

William Shakespeare

We Put the Fun in Dysfunction

My grandmother's father came from Ireland off the boat. Michael O'Neill was his name and he was a drunk. My grandmother's mother died when she was sixteen years old. She left my grandmother with five younger brothers; the youngest was five years old. When my grandmother got married to my grandfather, her five brothers and her father all moved in together with my grandfather.

My mother, Patricia, was born to Anne O'Neill Brown and Ken Brown. She was the first-born and had five younger siblings: three sisters, and two brothers. Since she was raised with her uncles, she was actually a middle child as well as the oldest. Her grandfather would get intoxicated and pass out on the front stoop of their home.

My mother would tell stories of being on a high school date and inviting her date inside, stepping over her father's body and saying, "Don't mind him." That made my grandmother a child of an alcoholic and my mother a child of an alcoholic. Therefore, it makes me and my three sisters "children of alcoholics." These were the days before Dr. Phil and Oprah. There was no recognition or realization of what that energy frequency did in their "life energy transactions" or the Karmic Pattern that was involved...

On my paternal grandparent's side, my grandfather also lost his mother when he was seven years old, so he, like my maternal grandmother, was a motherless child. People's Karmic Profiles will link together in patterns that can be "plugged-in" on both sides. Being a parentless child is definitely linked in within my personal Karmic Profile.

Just like my maternal grandmother, my paternal grandmother also had five siblings: four sisters and a brother. My father was the second child born to Lee N. Vail and Florence Tanner Vail. Even though he was small in stature, for most of his life, Dad was a star athlete. He was written up in the local newspapers for being a high school football and baseball star. He was also a scratch golfer and a bowler. My older cousin remembers watching him bowl a perfect game. Dad fought in World War II in the South Pacific and returned from the war at twenty-six years old with white hair. All his life, he suffered from post-traumatic stress syndrome. This was in the days before these conditions were recognized as an illness and treatment was not an option.

For most of my life, I remember Dad lying on the couch, very depressed. Actually, I know very little about his side of the family, since his father died while he was away in the war and his mother passed away when I was five years old. I do know there were Civil War soldiers in his background. I have a past life memory of being a Civil War soldier, which I will tell you about later. In our current profile we often reincarnate throughout the same family line.

Now remember, my mother was a child of an alcoholic. Her mother was very traumatized by the loss of her own mother and having to raise her siblings. And since my father suffered from PTSD, their energy frequency was the same. They vibrated in dysfunction, as it was part of their Karmic Profile. Therefore, when they got married, they were a "match made in heaven." They were soul mates.

Interesting how everyone is looking for their "soul mate." Your soul mate is the soul with whom you have incarnated many times to learn lessons with. I've been married to a soul mate at least twice, two different soul mates... and divorced them both! Soul mates can definitely be difficult for you.

From my perspective as a child, my parents had a non-communicative and non-loving relationship. Your childhood perspective may be different from that of your siblings, maybe due to your ages or birth order, but it is whatever you believe that counts for your own Karmic Profile.

My mother was very critical of her husband. She was also cold and closed-down. When I was an adult, she shared with me that being sandwiched between her uncles and her siblings caused her a great deal of difficulty. My grandmother would feed her brothers before the rest of the family. Whatever was left over was fed to my mother and her brothers and sisters.

One of my mother's uncles molested her when she was a child. She had a deep resentment toward men. Of course, as a child I would have no ability to understand that. From an adult perspective, I understand it intellectually; my inner child still feels the wounds of how I was raised. Those wounds will present themselves at various times in my own adult life. This is why it is so important for you to understand your own inner child issues. The inner child continues to reside within. With a snap of the fingers, the subconscious mind can rear its ugly head in the old, deeply etched Karmic Patterns!

Because of the story of my grandmother withholding food from her own children until her brothers ate, I understand the profile of eating disorders in my family. When my mother was pregnant with one of my sisters, she gained only five pounds. She said she only craved spinach and hard-boiled eggs. It was obviously much more than that. My sister was born a seven-pound baby. However, later on in her life, my sister struggled with anorexia. She received my mother's food belief system that translated through my mother's DNA and into the womb.

Thank goodness, my sister has now put Karmic challenge behind her. Throughout my life, however, I have struggled with using food as my choice to comfort myself emotionally. I still struggle with it, even though I have the knowledge of where it came from. It is imprinted within me and will continue to be a challenge. You see, because of what she had learned, for each meal, my mother cooked only enough food for our family to have just one helping.

As an adult I went in the opposite direction and overate to compensate. My children as well as many of my nieces and nephews have also struggled with weight issues. This stems from food issues in our Karmic Profile. Remember, the energetic transaction between who we are and what we think regarding what we have been taught, is a contributing factor to understanding our Karmic Profile.

I was raised as a third child of four girls. My older sister became very athletic like my father. My second sister went in the opposite direction and was very accident-prone. As understood by my childhood religiosity, I came in very spiritually oriented and self-sufficient. Without anyone directing me, I would make my bed every morning, I kept my room neat and tidy, and I always got straight A's in school. My youngest sister started seeing a psychiatrist when she was just a child; in 1964, this was unheard of.

My mother and father were "custodial parents" to me. A custodial parent puts a roof over your head, feeds you, gives you clothes, and your life. It looks like a life full of love but there's no real emotion coming from them. It took me years to figure out that when my mother brought tea and toast to my room in the morning before school, it was not a nurturing act. Rather, it was that she didn't want to have any conversation with me in the morning while she was having her coffee. She came disguised as a nurturer.

Because her mother (my grandmother) was an absentee mother (Grandma lost her mother and her hands were full taking care of her brothers), my mother was an absentee mother to me. It was a continuation of mother loss. This was another piece in the current Karmic Profile.

Now don't get me wrong—there were many happy times in my childhood. My mother and father did the best they could for who they were. This is not about parent bashing. It is about defining who you are from within. Nobody has a child, rocks them in their arms and says, "Oh, you're so cute... I'm gonna fuck you up." It just happens through the generations.

My father built us a cottage on a lake. We had amazing times at the lake, skiing, swimming and boating. My father had a strong work ethic that was transmitted to me and therefore to my children. My mother had a sharp wit and a wonderful sense of humor that was also passed on through the generations.

This is really about recognizing, understanding, realizing and processing appropriately who your parents were to you. You must do that in order for you to get to that level where you are going to understand your vibrational frequency, move into balance in your chakra system, and learn how to redefine yourself as a spiritual being rather than just somebody here on Earth meandering around life, wondering what the hell you're here for.

Let me take a moment and explain the word "chakra" to those of you who have never heard it before. "Chakra" is the Sanskrit word that means "energy wheel." The energy wheels in our body relate to the stages of human development. Your seven chakras begin at the root of your spine and move to the top of your head. According to Erik Erikson's theory of psychosocial development, we have eight stages of human development.

Erickson is best known for this theory as well as his concept of identity crisis. His theories created shifts in how we describe and understand personality and social influences. Despite having no formal academic degrees, Erikson taught at Harvard Medical school. He also published several books based on his theories and research, including *Childhood and Society* and the *The Life Cycle Completed.* His book, *Gandhi's Truth,* was awarded a Pulitzer Prize.

The chakras begin at the root or base of the spine, which relates to being at home in the world and in your body. The navel chakra relates to your sexuality and your creativity; the solar plexus chakra, to your willpower; the heart chakra, to giving and receiving love; the throat chakra, to communication; the third eye chakra, to perceptions into other worlds; and the crown chakra, to your heavenly connection, or your divine mind. The third eye and the crown chakra are the most readily and easily understood, as they are the most apparent in collective consciousness.

Our religious figures are depicted with halos above their heads. The halo symbolizes the high frequency energy or light that flows from their crown chakra or divine mind. Your mind is not within your brain. It resides outside of your body just above your head (like a hovercraft) and rides along with you through life.

Your mind is interrelated with the energy frequency of who you are through your past incarnations as well as life choices in your current Karmic Profile. This energy manifests as current time awareness, in partnership with the whole that you are in the Universe. Your brain is simply a giant computer bank that houses information, but it is your mind that accesses it. This is how we have free will, which we will discuss later in the book.

According to Erikson, the eight stages of psychosocial development are: infancy, which is age 0 to 23 months; early childhood, ages 2 to 4 years; preschool, ages 4 to 5 years; school-age, ages 5 to 12 years; adolescence, ages 13 to 19 years; early adulthood, ages 20 to 39 years; adulthood, ages 40 to 64 years; and maturity, which is age 65 to death.

The first seven stages coincide with the seven chakras and the death cycle. Erickson stipulates "wisdom" to be the "transactional analysis" or life review after your spirit leaves the "suitcase" (your body) and subsequently understands the amount of karmic "baggage" with which you are leaving the Earthly plane.

A thin line of energy that is circular in its motion connects the seven chakras. This is called Kundalini energy. That is why people who have had a Near Death Experience report going down a staircase or through a tunnel. When there is a trauma in life, or a perceived trauma (a trauma to one person may not be a trauma to another), it breaks the flow of the Kundalini.

When the Kundalini energy is broken, it transmits an electrical current or vibration to the Universe. The Universe is a giant mirror which reflects the trauma back through repetitive patterns in life. It is an energy that moves down through the generations and also places childhood data in the subconscious mind.

In order to understand this, the best exercise you can do is to create your own childhood timeline of events. Consider the things that you believed were trauma. Also, if possible, study your parents' and grandparents' lifelines and look for the patterns that emerge. If you want to have a happy life, you must not use your family's current profile as an excuse; it is only an explanation. At a soul level, failure to dig deeper means that you have chosen not to learn.

Therefore, happiness in part is accepting your chosen karmic footprint and making changes about the way you feel about your footprint. The Profile does not change, but your feelings do, and then the Law of Attraction will respond in kind.

Being true to yourself requires a great deal of emotional courage. The "truth" in you will be a continuous seeker, looking for the knowledge of your own inner truth, explored as a riddle borne in humility, and a lifetime filled with the quest of finding yourself.

If ever you meet someone who says they know completely the truth of who they are and have given up this quest, they have been fooled by their ego and are destined to repeat great Karma.

If we were to look to psychology for help, consider that the Greek word "psych" translates as "mind" and actually means "soul." Psychology in its purest sense means the understanding of the soul.

You are so much more than your consciousness. Your spirit is immensely more real and powerful than the thoughts that ruminate in your brain. If you try to heal your mind without engaging your soul, then you have set yourself up for a long, dark road of frustration.

In Their Own Words

My husband was diagnosed with a serious medical issue, but due to the nature of the illness, we had several months to make decisions about a treatment plan. I went to Melinda for a reading to see if she could offer any information that we had not already considered. Melinda knew exactly what we were dealing with, without my telling her anything and she helped me navigate through a difficult time. Melinda has been instrumental adding clarity to the family dynamics, allowing me to make healthy choices for myself. I also have recommended Melinda to friends and family that I felt would benefit from her help and most of them are long term clients as well.

—Sue

Act III

"We are such stuff as dreams are made on,
And our little life is rounded with a sleep."

William Shakespeare

The High School Football Star

So I told you that my name is Melinda Vail and that we are going to talk about both Melinda and Mindy. But actually my name at this stage of my life is Melinda Vail Gillette, Littlejohn, Kuhlman, Saine, Kronholm, and Larew. And yes, my current husband knows all of my history. So I want to dig a little deeper so you can see how my Karmic Profile ended up with so many marriages.

Remember that my mother was a child of an alcoholic. She had been molested, and was a custodial parent. My father was suffering from depression and post-traumatic stress disorder, angry that he once was a star athlete and was now living a life of mediocrity.

I was molested by a neighborhood teenager when I was ten. My mother focused on the two sisters who were on either side of me because they needed her more than I did. All of this information came into play in my adult relationships.

My first husband, John Gillette, and I attended the same high school. He was the star football quarterback. That made his energy like my father's. He was also a child of an alcoholic. His father could not hold down a job because he was so severely disabled by the alcohol. That made his energy like my mother's. When I was a sophomore in high school, I was what I would consider a nerd. I wore winged glasses on a chubby little face. Remember, this was in the late 1960s.

It was during my high school life that I began to understand that coincidences were actually synchronized energy. I did not put it in those terms then. I just realized that if something happened that looked coincidental, I would assign to it a designated fate. I saw such events occur around John.

I told several friends that I would marry John someday, and they laughed at me. Two years later, I shed my ugly duckling stage and turned into a swan. John and I began to date, which ended in my feelings being hurt when he stood me up for a high school prom. After John flunked out of college, he signed up for the Navy—this was at the tail end of the Vietnam War—so he wouldn't get drafted into the Army.

It was at that time that we began to reconnect. We started writing each other... and so it went. After getting together while he was on leave, we decided to marry. I got pregnant with my first child three months before the scheduled date of the wedding.

Since we were too young to legally marry, our parents had to sign for us. Remember, my parents were custodial parents, so it was easy for them to allow their eighteen-year-old child to be married. I had my first child before I turned nineteen. John's mother was difficult and he felt abandoned by her. Once again, the energy was a perfect vibrational frequency for the generations of my Karmic Profile.

Because he felt so insecure from his childhood, John was a serial cheater. My subconscious mind did what it was taught in my childhood. I got sick. I had several major surgeries during the time we were married. After all, isn't that how my two sisters got my mother's attention? My subconscious mind taught me that to get John's attention, I must compete with another woman. The formula inside of me that included the energetic dynamics of my generational patterns and upbringing was now being cemented in my first marriage.

After eleven very difficult, challenging, emotionally debilitating years and two more children, John and I got divorced. The final straw was when he had yet another affair with one of his co-workers while I was pregnant with our third child. The prior three years had been rough.

In July of 1979, I had my second child by Caesarian section. In July of 1980, I had a very bad gallbladder attack, which resulted in surgery and a three-week hospital stay. In July of 1981, I had my daughter by C-section. Enough was enough! When my daughter was just six weeks old, I left John and got a job waitressing, to support my children.

Two very positive energetic transactions occurred during the time John and I were together. Since they affected me in a positive way, I would like to mention them as well.

The first transaction was when John and I were newly married in 1973 and had an old "beater with a heater" car. We were traveling from our hometown in upstate New York back to John's duty station in Philadelphia and had only enough money in our pockets to throw into the toll booth at the Walt Whitman Bridge so we could get back to our apartment in New Jersey.

We had pulled into a rest stop for a break and to our dismay, our car would not re-start. John returned to the rest stop building to make a phone call for help and I waited in the car with our son, who was still an infant. What a dilemma, stuck in the middle of nowhere... I started to cry.

Two men got out of a car that was parked next to ours. One of them asked me, "What's the matter, Lady? Why are you crying?" They were "New York City New Yorkers" and the man who'd spoken had a crusty edge to his voice.

I answered through my tears that our car had broken down and we didn't know how we were going to get home. They looked under the hood of the car and discovered the problem was a dead battery. Returning to their car, they pulled out a brand-new battery and installed it in our car in place of the dead one.

"There you go, Lady. Have a great day!" Driving off, they disappeared into the night.

I was too young and naïve, dumbfounded perhaps, to even ask for names to reimburse them. It was a random act of kindness that I will never forget. After 44 years, I still hold in my heart much gratitude for those two men.

The second act of human kindness occurred after I had left John. I was visiting my obstetrician for my sixth-week C-section check-up and when my doctor asked how I was doing, I burst into tears and told him the story of discovering that John had been cheating.

When I went to pay my bill, the nurse said, "The Doctor says to tell you that he has taken care of this for you." Once again, I will never forget the kindness of that man.

These two random acts of kindness were examples of how truly spiritual people know how to behave in life. Through those energetic transactions I have learned to be a very generous, charitable human being.

Now let me give you my share of the responsibility in the marriage with John. Remember that my mother was very critical of my father. Because I saw her treat him that way, I "believed" that was the way one loved their husband. Remember, if a woman is raised in a household where the father beats the mother up, she says, "I'm never going to marry a man like my father." But statistically that's exactly what she does. It becomes her belief system that was created from within her subconscious mind.

My example led me to be highly critical of John. Because his mother also put him down, many times in our marriage, the way I was "loving him" drove him further away from me and into the arms of someone else. He was trying to find love in his own way. Also, remember I was molested, as was my mother, so there was a basic energy of disliking and mistrusting men that played into our dynamics. I also shut down our sex life and continued using food to nurture myself. I would get fat, then thin and then fat, and thin... over and over, as a form of self-abuse. If I was shutting down and abusing myself, was it any wonder that I attracted it into our marriage and that John was doing the same?

You must look at all angles when you're trying to understand your Karmic Profile—not just with what you attracted in a relationship, but also, what your role and responsibility were in the exchange of energy in that relationship. In addition, it's not only the negative things that you're supposed to understand and learn from, but also, the positive energy that should create who you are in the Now.

In Their Own Words

Melinda Vail is a gifted hypnotherapist and intuitive therapist. I have had the pleasure of having her take me through childhood regression therapy numerous times. I am a fifty-one-year-old woman who has gone to more than five other therapists since adulthood. Although they were helpful, they never got me to

the point of not repeating old patterns. Usually we could identify the patterns but not break them or clear them. Regression
therapy has enabled me to go from working for an unreason-
able person to landing a job with a wonderful boss. I was sur-
prised at how easily I could let go, trust, and thus allow Melinda
to hypnotize me. Being hypnotized is much like meditating; it is
very relaxing and easy. I am sure this is due to Melinda being
very gentle, loving, giving, and caring. She makes one feel at
ease very quickly. She used her other gifts of intuition and mediumship to enhance the therapy sessions and always hit the nail
on the head for me. She is a sincere and generous person who
I am honored to know and simply recommend so highly! She is
a find!!!

—Jennie

Act IV

"To thine own self be true."

William Shakespeare

Nice Guys Finish Last

After leaving John, I was supporting three children on a waitress's wage. I was twenty-nine years old, a single mother with an eight-year-old, a two-year-old, and an infant. Several of the young men who came into the restaurant flirted with me and I ended up marrying one of them. Casey worked at IBM and in my eyes, this meant he was stable. My sister had told me that no man would want to be with a woman with three young children. This was in 1981.

So when this nice, kind, stable young man came along, I made a logical decision to marry him. I felt his loving me was going to be enough for me, even though I did not return the favor in the same way. In that same year, I had a baby, got divorced and got remarried—all in one year!

Casey was probably too functional for me, even though some of his background fit the Karmic Profile. He had been abandoned by his mother and was raised by a grandmother; again, there was the abandoned child syndrome.

It was during that time that I was drawn to metaphysics. In 1973, when I was still married to John, we went to the theater to see *The Exorcist.* It scared me to death! Throughout my life, psychic things had occurred and I had always just taken them for granted. When I was a child, I had an imaginary friend; I called her Stony. My mother was very good about it and would even set a place at our dinner table for her. So my mother taught me that it was okay to talk to someone no one else could see.

The movie shut all of that down and crept into my deeply implanted fears about the devil from a Catholic perspective. Early in our marriage when John was a Navy corpsman and worked the hospital graveyard shift, I had to have another corpsman come to the house and stay with me because I was afraid.

During the year when we first separated, John's father died. He was the first spirit that ever came to me after death and he gave me a message for John. John did not believe it. However, this experience opened me up to be able to connect to the other side.

In my marriage with Casey, I had time to study metaphysics. I took an automatic writing class and connected with an Angel called Zarah.

I met a man who channeled and began to really get into what energy means on this planet. As I pursued a level of understanding, I recognized that I did not love Casey and told him that I had made a mistake and wanted a divorce. We were married less than a year.

The truth was that I was still in love with John and wished to reconcile with him. However, he had decided to marry the co-worker with whom he had had an affair. I was divorced from Casey when John married his new wife. He asked Casey to be his best man. What Karmic irony that my first ex-husband asked my second ex-husband to stand up for him at his second wedding!

John had a fourth child with his new wife. When she needed to have a hysterectomy, John asked me to babysit her three children plus their new baby so he could be at her side in the hospital. Of course, that's what I did because love does not go away when you really love someone.

I spent the next four years being alone and on my own with my children. It was a constant struggle to take care of three kids, put food on the table, and keep a roof over our heads. Out of circumstance, I became a custodial parent. And that was to repeat the Karmic energy from my grandmother to my mother, from my mother to me, and from me to my children. As Sonny and Cher would say "*...and the beat goes on...*"

In Their Own Words

Hi Melinda!

You did a reading on my friend Megan and I've been great friends with her for over twenty years. We have exchanged birthday gifts every year since we have known each other. She said hands down, you were the best gift I have ever gotten her and it was the best gift she has ever received! Wow!!! Just wanted to thank you!

Xoxo

—Jenny

Act V

"Nothing will come of nothing."

William Shakespeare

The Man & The Mill

I moved to Louisville, Kentucky for a brief time because my sister lived there and I went to work for my brother-in-law in a jewelry store that he owned. I discovered that not only did I not like Louisville but also, I did not like my brother-in-law.

I ended up quitting my job at the jewelry store. I went to college during the day and waitressed the graveyard shift at Denny's. It was a struggle for me. I depended on my oldest child, Jason, to help out immensely.

One Christmas Eve, I was cooking dinner and discovered I was missing one ingredient. The grocery store was just down the street, so I tucked some money into my jeans pocket and popped my baby daughter into her car seat, leaving my two boys at home. Off I went to get what I needed.

One block from my home, a policeman pulled me over. I had New York tags on my car and he claimed that my car was a stolen vehicle. He called in back-up and soon I was surrounded by two other police cars. I was scared to death as the officer had threatened that he would take my child to child protective services. Of all times to have merely put some money into my jeans pocket and driven off without my identification, vehicle license, or registration!

After putting me through a huge ordeal, the officer gave me his name and phone number on a piece of paper, winked at me and told me if I called him, he would forget about the whole thing. Later, when I was working at Denny's, another officer shared with me that I should stay away from that policeman because he was dangerous. He must have been right. The "dangerous" officer would drive back and forth in front of my house; he knew where I lived because of course, I had given him my address when he'd stopped me.

This guy gave me the greatest gift I've ever received in my life! Spirit says, "Honor the jackasses in your life"; they can give you the most, or will be your greatest teachers. Because of my fear of what was going on, my dad retired early from his job to help me and my children move from Louisville back to Upstate New York where I had received a job offer. He stayed with me for six months and I was no longer a custodial parent.

My father was hands-on and helped me manage my life and children. During his stay with us, the house had been accidentally locked and he didn't have a key. When he tried to break through a second-story window, he fell from a ladder and broke his pelvic bone. He ended up extending his visit and recovering in a hospital bed that we placed in my living room.

My father and I were able to break the Karmic Patterns that had manifested in our lives. Our relationship became that of a father and daughter as well as a grandfather who cared for his grandchildren. This is the reason I consider the accident an incredible gift.

Shortly after my father recovered from the fall, he returned to his home in Florida and was diagnosed with aplastic anemia. He was given six months to live.

Because my father so loved the game of golf and being on the golf course, I think he actually extended his time on earth and made it for almost two more years. Because of that policeman, I was able to complete all Karma with my dad. When Dad left, I felt like we had done what we needed to do in each other's lives. After he passed away and he began to give me signs that he was with me, I became increasingly more open to understanding life after life.

Before my dad died, I met my third husband, Walter Kuhlman. Walter's Karmic Profile was different. He had a wonderful family and great parents. They welcomed me and my children with open arms. I finally felt like I had a family connection. They were very religious, actually practicing their faith and not just preaching it. However, I soon realized they were not at all what they were cracked up to be. Religion was their cover for dysfunction.

Walter owned his own mill company where he made hardwood flooring, crown molding, and other types of trim for contractors. One day when we were not yet married and were still just dating, a piece of wood flew out of a machine, stabbed Walter in the stomach and perforated his intestine. He was hospitalized and had to have surgery, so he asked me to step in and help him at the mill. I gave up my apartment and moved into his home. The house and the mill were on the same property, so it was convenient. By that time, my two youngest children were in first and third grade and my oldest was in junior high.

Then, the bottom fell out of the real estate market (still in the Eighties) and Walt lost his business. By that time, we were married and Walt had not fully recovered from his injury. Since he had never been trained for any business other than running his mill, this threw him into a depression. I ended up being the breadwinner in our family. It felt like I was not being taken care of, and my abandonment issues and fears of not having enough or being enough kicked in.

So... of course, I criticized Walt. I was trying to motivate him through criticism because that's what I had learned. Also, I comforted myself yet again with food, and detached physically. I was repeating the patterns of my first marriage. Walt also repeated some of his patterns and ran away. When he was younger he ran away to the Peace Corps to avoid being drafted. This time he ran away to New York City and went missing. At once we called the NYC Police Department and filed a missing report.

Walt put his family and me through hell for several days before the NYCPD called to tell us he was in New York with a woman. I was devastated. The patterns of cheating repeated once again. I packed up what I could from my home, gathered as much money as I could scrape together by hook or by crook, grabbed up my children, and moved to Arizona.

My sister lived in Phoenix and after my father died, my mother had moved to Arizona to be close to her. When Jason, my oldest, graduated from high school, he also moved to the Phoenix area to be with us.

At thirty-nine years old and with two kids in tow, I drove cross-country to the Southwest to begin a new life.

While I was married to Walter, I continued my quest for spiritual knowledge and did some hypnosis to understand myself better. I connected with a group of women who were clairvoyant and supposedly able to get messages from the other side. I also read many metaphysical books. For the most part, I found spiritual people disappointing;

they were a dysfunctional group. I connected with one man, a chan-
neler, who turned out to be a molester. I told myself that just as religions teach us, spirituality is a bad thing to be involved in. My energy
transactions with people in this field had turned into skepticism, cyni-
cism, and incredulity.

After I arrived in Arizona, I got a job selling advertising to business
owners. In Upstate New York, I had been an advertising executive with
several publications; this was my area of expertise. One day as I was
passing a metaphysical store called The Peace of the Universe, the little
voice in my head that had talked to me so often throughout my life told
me if I stopped there, the owner would buy an ad. I was one ad short of
making my quota for a paycheck—once again I was a custodial parent
working long hours to put a roof over my children's head. That paycheck would help out substantially.

Sure enough, the owner, Judy, was a very nice lady. Judy said to me
that "Spirit" had told her I was a very good person. She said if I would
read a certain book, she would buy an ad from me. She knew if I prom-
ised I would read the book, I would. Judy paid for the ad and I read the
book. It was titled *The Celestine Prophecy,* written by James Redfield.
Little did I know that three years later, James and I would speak at the
same spiritual event!

The next week, I was stuck once more for an ad. Once again, the
voice told me to go see Judy, so off I went. Again, Judy bartered a deal
with me. She said, "I would like you to join a meditation group that is

upstairs from this bookstore and I will give you another ad." As before, I honored my agreement and attended the event with my mother in tow.

It was here that the light bulb came on. We were all doing psychometry, a metaphysical process whereby you hold an object of someone else's that contains the energy of that person.

I was holding a pen. Most of the other attendees were just saying nice things to each other, such as: "I see a beach around you," or, "I think you are a very nice person." I was seeing two white standard poodles and Elvis Presley. I gathered my courage to say what I felt, saw, and heard.

At once, the woman whose object I was holding in my hand began to cry and said, "That was my husband's. He collected Elvis memorabilia and we have two white standard poodles. He died a few months ago."

The whole room was hushed for what felt like an eternity to me. Finally, my mother piped up and said, "Good for you, Mindy. Good for you!" And that's how we started.

Now I knew I could speak to the dead. As I look back on it, I am extremely grateful to Walter for behaving so badly. If he hadn't run away to another woman, I would not have come to Arizona. I would not have been able to make the connections that would lead me toward what I am able to do now. Our marriage and its contract, the subsequent pain that we caused each other, led me to a place where I could find my higher power. I learned to help other people connect in ways in which they were reassured that their loved ones were alive.

I have one more story about Walter, but I will leave that to Act X, when we are talking about Akashic Records.

In Their Own Words

I visit with Melinda to speak to my wife and other family members who have passed. It has given me a great pleasure and peace of mind to communicate with them. There is no question for me that I am speaking with my loved ones. The greatest confirmation of Melinda's abilities is from the dozens of people I have referred to her over the years, including my personal physician, professional associates, family and friends. To the most skeptical, I offer to reimburse the full cost of their session with Melinda if they are in any way unhappy. All have expressed amazement at Melinda's abilities and are grateful for the referral. No one has ever asked for a refund!

—Bart

Act VI

"There is nothing either good or bad,
But thinking makes it so."

William Shakespeare

If the Name Fits

After beginning to understand that I could give readings and talk to people who were dead, I decided to get certified in hypnosis. During my training, I learned that I had a real talent and natural ability to see the energy around somebody's life. I could also see their Karmic Profile. I did not connect the two or recognize it as such until many years later.

In 1994, I began practicing as a working clairvoyant, medium and hypnotherapist, and for the past 23 years, I have had a thriving practice. Even during the recession, I was booked many weeks and months in advance.

You might think that because I was doing so well and helping so many people, my own life Karma would settle down. Ahhh, don't be fooled by Karma! Your Karma is still your profile, no matter what you do for work. What you do and who you are can be two different things.

That brings me to husband number four, who was Dick. I have always joked that Dick's mother was psychic when he was born, because of the name she chose for him. Not only did he come from a drinking family, but he himself was a functional alcoholic. He fit right into my Karmic Profile; we were a match made in heaven.

By this time, my children were in their late teens or already out of high school. Dick had two daughters of his own, ages eight and ten. I was swept off my feet by his ability to wine and dine me. For the first time in my life, I had a partner who wasn't depending on me to be the breadwinner.

I felt, however, that Dick still had an attachment not only to the mother of his children, but also to another ex-wife, with whom he spoke frequently. Even this fit right into my subconscious profile of competing with another woman to get attention. In my opinion, Dick had a serious enmeshment with his mother as well. Nevertheless, he was fun and he taught me how to have nice things, how not to work so hard, to enjoy vacations, and to play in life.

On the down side, Dick tried to separate me from my family. He tried to get me to quit my job so I could work with him. He wanted me to totally enmesh my life with his.

Dick hated that I was well known in my business. Sometimes we would be out and someone would ask him what it felt like to be married to me. They called him "Mr. Vail." That does not make a narcissist happy. Constantly he pressured me to close down my practice.

One time when we were about to leave for a vacation at Lake Powell, I had an opportunity to meet with one of Oprah's representatives. Dick refused to delay our departure until after the meeting. He gave me a choice... my career or him. I chose to go with him because I had been married so many times before. I was embarrassed as this was my fourth marriage. My ego was involved.

I was not listening to the signals the Universe was giving me. Instead, Mindy, my inner child, was working hard at being loved. Also, I really felt like I loved Dick and I also felt like I loved his children. I felt spending time with them had given me a second chance to enjoy children. This desire was in response to the years when I was raising my own three children and was so unavailable to them. I wanted to be more than a custodial parent... I had an inner desire to break that Karmic Pattern.

When one of Dick's children was in her late teens, she was very challenged with some addiction issues. My daughter and I were her advocates and tried to do everything we could to help her, but her parents were reluctant participants because of the dysfunction in their own lives. It put a huge stress on our marriage. Eventually we broke.

Same tune, different verse.

Dick became enamored with someone else and made it very clear to me how he felt. Of course, I did my usual pull-back physically, because I had gained weight.

We visited a variety of counselors but nothing seemed to help. By this time, my mother clearly had dementia, which created additional stress, as we put her in an assisted living home. So, between a child that was challenged with addiction and a mother who was in the early stages of dementia, and keeping my practice afloat without any signs to my clientele of the stress I was under, I chose to leave the marriage.

And another one bites the dust. What I learned through this relationship was not to give up on myself and be engulfed by another. Forfeiting my opportunity with Oprah was enough. I wasn't going to give away the entirety of who I was to someone who would not appreciate it. Leaving this marriage was an emancipation proclamation for my soul... I was sure I would attract better next run. Now I was fifty-four years old and had been married four times.

In Their Own Words

Before I met Melinda, I was swimming in a mental world of "what if's" and "I wonder what that's like?" I have always been a Spiritual soul, but never met anyone who took me by the hand for a walk on "The Other Side."

After a suggestion from a friend, I made an appointment with Melinda somewhere around '97 or '98. My husband had passed over in August '95 and I was totally lost at that point. I wasn't sure who I was, or what tomorrow would bring. Our two grown daughters had their own children and lives, and so I began to learn to walk alone.

At our first meeting, Melinda was able to make contact with my husband Gary immediately for me, and that brought peace to my being. The messages she was able to pass to me gave me dates and names of events/people that only Gary and I knew. Just to know that he was fine, happy, and actually by my side was so comforting. Her common-sense approach has helped me to have the courage to look inward and listen. Melinda has taught me to trust my intuitions; they will always be true to you.
—Joan

Act VII

"The course of true love never did run smooth."

William Shakespeare

The Colonel & The Clairvoyant

I met Ed through Match.com. After Dick and I split up, I was doing well in my life. I had my own home and things were great with my work. My daughter was happily married and my boys were doing fine. I was in a relatively happy place, but I felt like I wanted to meet someone to spend some time with, and have companionship.

When I met Ed, I did the very same thing as when I married Casey. I made a conscious choice to get together with someone for whom there was no great love. Ed was just a good, kind, caring person. It felt to me like we could spend time together without all the drama.

Soon after Ed and I met, Jason, my oldest child, developed an abscess in his liver. When they proceeded to drain the abscess, his heart and lungs gave out. He ended up in ICU on a ventilator, in a coma for almost three weeks. I almost lost him.

After he was in recovery, Jason needed to stay with me for the next six weeks because he had to be given antibiotics by IV every day at the hospital on an outpatient basis. It was extremely difficult to get him to the hospital every day while I was working.

Ed worked from home so he offered to transport Jason back and forth to the hospital. To make it easier and more convenient for every-one, he also offered to have Jason stay with him. It was an extremely unselfish, generous thing for him to do. Indeed, it clinched it for me that I should be with someone who would do something so magnanimous.

We never lived with each other before we married. That was defi-nitely my mistake. Once again, my Karmic Profile reared its ugly head. Ed had been a bachelor for a long time and he had certain ways of doing things that conflicted with a partnership. He would forget that he was married and do things on his own without even a second thought about it. It was as if I were invisible at times, and once again, I found myself in a custodial situation.

We had been married less than six months when Ed began to get ill. He had physical limitations that created an inability for us to be inti-mate, which of course fit into my Karmic Profile. I limited my own physical connections when I was upset in the marriage. I also used food as a substitute and got fat again.

At age fifty-nine, Ed was diagnosed with Alzheimer's. Sometime later, the Alzheimer's diagnosis was amended to temporal frontal lobe dementia. However, the CT scan showed no compromise in the frontal lobe. He was a brittle diabetic and sometimes diabetes can affect brain function as well.

At this stage, we didn't know what was going on. Ed would repeat questions over and over, he would get angry for no particular reason, and he would say and do inappropriate things. The truth was, we had not been married long enough. I felt like I was living with and taking care of my Dutch uncle.

I was doing just great in my practice helping lots of people, but in my personal life, I felt desperately unhappy. It made me feel angry and critical. Frankly, I think I was as difficult for him as he was for me. Of course, my Karmic Profile was present in this relationship as well. Shortly after we got together, Ed could no longer work. I was, yet again, the main working breadwinner, although he had income from his Army pension as well as savings. Our house was old, the property was large, and it took a great deal of money to maintain it. As I modernized the house, I went through most of my own savings.

Ed had been abandoned by his biological father and was raised by an alcoholic stepfather. He had both the energy frequencies of an aban-doned child and a child of an alcoholic. Ed was also very attached to his former wife whom he had put through medical school. He resented that shortly after she became a doctor, she left him. This fit into everything that was part of all the energies that were present throughout the other relationships in my life.

I seriously thought my life was over. I would have stayed with Ed forever, except for the Universe giving me a wonderful break. His former high school girlfriend emailed me and asked if she could come for a visit while she was visiting her grandchildren in Phoenix. I encouraged her to stay with us and that is what she did.

Before I came along, Ed's dream in his retirement was to drive around with his Airstream trailer in tow and go from beach to beach and place to place. Because he had this dream and because he was still in a place where he could do it mentally, I suggested that since the big house was now too expensive for us to afford, we should sell it. I would rent a place where he could stay with me when he was back in town.

I thought that was our plan. Imagine my surprise when I discovered that he and his girlfriend from high school were taking a cross-country trip together. Needless to say, I was extremely hurt and very angry by her choice to take advantage of the situation.

Honestly, looking back on it, she was yet another person who did something wonderful for me by coming into my life. Even though it looked like it was a negative at the time, I am so grateful to her because she freed me from a burdensome marriage. As of this writing, I am not even sure if he is with her and if he has dementia or Alzheimer's. He seems to be getting along just fine as he stays in touch with my son-in-law, for the sake of our grandson.

I'm not sure what his behavior in our relationship was about. There was a disturbing diagnosis, unusual and difficult patterns in our domestic life, and the failure of trust and respect. Looking back, I choose to let it all go and be a part of another lesson learned.

In Their Own Words

Melinda is amazing... she not only has given me spot on readings, but has also done hypnosis with me to do past life regression and childhood analysis. Melinda has worked with me on counseling and honest, straight-to-the-point advice, which helped me in both my personal and professional life. Thank you for your caring and kindness.

—Allison

Act VIII

*"Love looks not with the eyes, but with the mind.
And therefore is winged Cupid painted blind."*

William Shakespeare

Harley & Me

This is a short chapter because it is about the man I am married to now. Yes, number six has got to be It for me.

Our story begins with my giving a seminar in Sedona last year (2016). I had been single for three years, living blissfully alone and enjoying my tribe of friends, travel, work, and being content. I still carried some of the weight from my marriage to Ed as protection not to get involved with another man... at least not physically.

I was spending some time with a dear male friend who served as a person who could go with me on dates and trips with no pressure. I have really bonded with my grandson, Elliot, and have spent much time with him. It feels so good to be able to do that. Elliot is a Crystal Child. Crystal children are emotionally and spiritually mature. They are here to save our butts on this planet—which we desperately need.

Elliot says things that knock my socks off. When Carrie Fisher died, he said to me, "Grandma, did you hear that Princess Leah died?"

I replied, "Yes honey, I heard that."

"Why did she die, Grandma?"

I took this moment as a way to teach Elliot about drugs, telling him that she wore her heart out by taking drugs and drinking alcohol; so when she died, she was younger than Grandma. I also said to him, "A day later, her mother died."

"Really?" he said. Then he smiled broadly. "That's great! Now they can be together in heaven." Out of the mouths of babes, my eight-year-old sage!

My work had become more developed and my connection with Spirit continued to be very steady and strong. I was in a good place as I prepared for that Sedona seminar. At the time, the man whom I now know as "Billy" and who called himself "Amadeus" had a Welcome Center in Sedona. It was a place where people would post flyers and information for their businesses and real estate.

I walked into the Welcome Center with a woman who was helping to promote my event and she introduced me to Billy. The first words out of his mouth were, "You make me vibrate."

While we were returning to the car, the promoter asked me, "What was that?"

"I don't know," I said.

In truth, when I first heard Billy's name, I got a hit of energy similar to the first time I saw my first husband.

Billy was invited by the event promoters to come to the seminar. On stage, a co-presenter was doing an exercise in which she led the audience to partner up with a person and then look into each other's eyes to make an energetic connection.

The only seat available was the one next to Billy. I could hardly contain myself when I looked into his eyes and jabbered on about what I was picking up about him psychically. He just quietly nodded his head.

At the end of the exercise, the presenter asked if anyone would like to share. I raised my hand and blurted out that they almost lost a speaker that night because we were going to go get a room.

When it was my turn on stage, I was doing readings that connected people to their loved ones on the other side. After the seminar, Billy came up to me and said, "Now I know that this can be done." That was in June.

In August, I went to Mexico with my tribe. We all had a very good time. While I was there, I received an email from Billy asking if he could come for lunch and a reading. My schedule is very hectic and the time he requested was unavailable. I offered another time and he quickly accepted.

When he came for lunch and the reading, it was like electricity was going through both of us. It was the most energetic connection and transaction that I have ever had with anyone in my life. After the reading, I emailed him and asked him what was going on. The problem was, he was married and it had been a 25-year marriage. After all the times I had been hurt by men who were married to me and went out with other women, I would never date a married man.

Ten days later, I went to Sedona for work. Billy and I ended up having a conversation where we agreed that we felt love for each other, love at first sight. He had the difficult task of explaining it to his wife, who actually handled it graciously.

Billy moved into my house without our ever having a date or even kissing. Little did I know that he rode a Harley-Davidson and once was the leader of a pack! He also was the mayor of his town in Texas. He likes to wear his hair long in a ponytail, has a dry sense of humor, and is one hell of a cook. I jokingly tell him he is Julia Child by day and "Fabio" by night! He just laughs.

Unbelievably, we are matched perfectly and have lived harmoniously and happily since that day. Now, how does that fit into the current profile? Well, his mother died when he was five years old, so he is indeed a motherless child. When he first came into my life, he would have one too many drinks in the evening, which he has subsequently stopped.

The difference in this relationship is that between us, we can actually communicate all of our past as well as our backgrounds. We are sincerely trying to understand what our paths have been in our Karmic Profile and to make sure that our energetic transactions occur with integrity and honor for the gift that the Universe gave us in finding each other.

We have been a hundred percent honest in what triggers us. We have absolutely been working toward a connection that does not include all of the old issues that we were both taught. Only time will tell. But, so far so good, even as he has stepped into my business to manage it and we are together 24/7. Fingers crossed.

In Their Own Words

I recently had a reading with Melinda. I did not know exactly what to expect. Wow, did I ever get information that made me think about my loved ones. She was accurate on so many things. Melinda is so kind and understanding. I need to come back sometime soon and go into deeper levels of understanding. Thank you, Melinda, for all you give to each of us. You are a very special person and a blessing to everyone you meet.

—Sharon

Act IX

"We know what we are,
But know not what we may be."

William Shakespeare

What Does It All Mean?

F irst and foremost, healing your Karmic Profile is in part simply identifying it—but once you have identified it, that does not mean it goes away. It is still a part of the essence of what you've chosen, coming into the world. It is still part of your energy and will always be until you die.

By understanding and recognizing the hidden and subtle energies that cause patterns in your life and understanding the behavioral attributes associated with those patterns, you can find your soul purpose within your chosen life lessons and experiences.

Everyone asks me, "What is my life's purpose?" and the answer is always the same. Your life's purpose is to figure out what you've chosen to learn before you reach the other side and have your "life review," which can best be understood as a *transactional analysis*.

If you can understand your purpose and figure out what you've chosen as your essence, then you are "unpacking the baggage" in this lifetime. This gives your soul essence the opportunity to move into a different frequency of energy when you are choosing your next incarnation.

This acknowledgement enhances your life with a deeper understanding of who you are and hopefully helps you to find the emotional courage to make changes. When you rationally process your Karmic Profile, it gives your life's challenges a new meaning and deeper understanding. You can enrich your life to a new level of introspection and release patterns into the "neutral zone."

The opposite of love is not hate. The opposite of love is neutral. We are looking to be neutral about our experiences here on the earth plane so that we can be in a state of gratitude, graciousness and grace.

I am so grateful to all the men I have loved in my life, and every lesson that each marriage taught me.

I am also grateful to my mother and father as well as my sisters, for always doing the best they could, within their own Karmic Profile.

Most of all, I am grateful that I have found within me the ability to connect with my Spirit, so I can begin to decipher my own Karmic Profile—to move in a direction in which my spiritual journey will complete itself on this earth and transition to another form of energy.

Perhaps my future is to be among the stars, or wherever else my imagination can take me.

What is it that I have learned through it all? First, I've learned that I am enough. That I count. That one way or another, because we are all born to human beings, sometimes we all feel like a motherless child.

I have learned that I don't need to compromise my integrity or my values to find love. That I can be honest with myself and look myself in the mirror and still honor who I am—that I don't have to give myself up just because I want a relationship. There is no competition except for the competition that we have within ourselves. It's okay for me to kick ass and take names.

I have learned that sharing my duality empowers me and others. I have no fear to share it. My role in life is to help others, and my difficult experiences have given me a better ability to do that. Within that role, I don't need to be afraid of my greatness. Comparing yourself with someone else is an exercise in futility.

I could go on and on. I hope that after you read this book you will process your life's challenges with new meaning—that you will surrender to your mastering negative patterns and co-create with the Universe to spring you forward into a deeper connection with yourself.

The *Wizard of Oz* represents everything we seek as human beings. We're all trying to find our "brain," our "heart," and our "courage." We all want to find our way home. It is our life's purpose to discover how we seek to understand our specific Karmic Profile.

The Wicked Witch is of course the shadow in us all, misleading us to seek power as the path to happiness. The Wizard is her ego, hiding behind a curtain and pulling the strings.

With just a tap of our shoes, we can banish the bad dream because we have always had the power to get back to ourselves. When the Wicked Witch etched "surrender Dorothy" across the sky, it represented our own need to yield, for it is in the surrender, not the struggle, that we find our way.

In fact, we must acquiesce to our "shadow side" in order to let it go! When a man struggles in quicksand he will sink. If he remains in peace, he will stay on the surface long enough for someone to offer a branch to pull him out. Trust and the Universe will provide all the answers. Recognize the Karma you've chosen, as that is the first step in self-awareness.

In Their Own Words

Thank God for Melinda! My name is Karen. I am a retired realtor. After the death of my son to suicide in April 2010, I was devastated—I couldn't focus. His death consumed me. A friend recommended I visit Melinda. After my first "session" with her, I was hooked. I can honestly say she helped save my life. I've had great support from my husband and daughter but my sessions with Melinda have enabled me to see through my tears and feel hope. With her help, I am learning how to connect with my son. I am more aware of my surroundings and the Spirit World. Little things I took for granted, I now notice. I highly recommend anyone who needs clarity, guidance, and direction for whatever your level of need, to make an appointment with Melinda. It can't hurt.

—*Karen*

Act X

"The evil that men do lives after them;
The good is oft interred with their bones."

William Shakespeare

Akashic Records

The Akashic Record or the "Book of Life" is said to be the Universe's super-computer system. It is supposed to be the storehouse of all the information for every individual who has ever lived on Earth. It contains within it all the thoughts, words, feelings or intentions that have occurred at any time in the history of the world.

The Universe is like a giant energetic mirror reflecting back to us whatever we put out to it. Our thoughts, our words, our feelings and our intentions create an accountability factor when interchanging energy with the Universe.

Edgar Casey (1877-1945), known as the "Sleeping Prophet," often talked about these records. He claimed to do his readings by tapping into the Akashic Records and his subject's subconscious minds. The accuracy of Casey's psychic work is well documented.

Many times I have clients who have no obvious patterns in their Karmic Profile from current life circumstances but still have seemingly impossible challenges. If you cannot find the reasons for that duality within nature or nurture, then you have to go back and look at the Akashic Record. Sometimes there's some inner knowledge from a past life, an inner knowing that you were at some place in time, or maybe it's a historical event or certain country that you're drawn to.

I would like to go back to some of the amazing things that my grandson Elliot has said. When he was about three and we were in the back seat of my son-in-law and daughter's car together, he told me, "Grandma, when I was in my Mom's belly I was on an airplane." That was true; my daughter had flown to Colorado when she was pregnant with him.

I asked him, "Elliot, how do you know that?"

"Because I heard the engine," he said. Following up on that remark, he stated very matter-of-factly, "When I was a daddy man, we used to jump out of airplanes, but something kept me from being killed when I touched the ground."

I asked, "Was it called a parachute?"

He slapped his little knee and exclaimed, "That's it, a parachute!"

I decided I would ask him additional questions. "Elliot, were you in Vietnam?" He said no, he wasn't. I asked another question: "Elliot, were you in World War II?"

"That's it!" he said. "I was in World War II."

We took him to Hawaii at age five and he was fascinated by its history. He couldn't get enough of it. Now at eight years old, he still holds a fascination with World War II and even reads thick books. This is something beyond the norm for most second graders.

When my daughter was in second grade, which was before the movie *Schindler's List* came out, she described to me the inside of a gas chamber. All her lifelong friends are Jewish and they were in her wedding party.

From the time my son McKennan was seven years old, he was a champion wrestler. His career came to an abrupt halt at age 16, when he severely injured his knee and could no longer wrestle. I told him, "Go meditate about it and see why you manifested this injury."

He went into his room for about an hour and when he emerged, he said to me, "I was in Vietnam, Mom, and I got my leg blown off at the knee. No one could get to me and I lay there and bled to death. I do not want to be drafted in this lifetime."

Interesting, how he has come into this life with some post-trauma. As an infant, he was premature and had a bubble in his lung. The pediatrician gave him a 50/50 chance to live. Ailments to lungs mean grief, so he came into this life still grieving his last incarnation. He is also the child who has wrestled with clinical depression during this lifetime. He was my father's favorite grandchild, so it is no surprise that they would resonate with the same energy.

When I was studying to be a past life regression hypnotherapist, we hypnotized each other for practice. Under hypnosis, I described a lifetime where I was with a brother who had gone with the Confederacy and I had gone with the Union. I was angry with him for his choices and when we were on the battlefield together, helplessly I watched him get killed.

A cannon ball landed near my leg and blew my leg off at the knee. When I returned to my farm in Pennsylvania, I sat on the porch in a rocking chair all day in a state of depression, while my wife and children worked the farm. When the therapist asked me if the brother whom I watched die had incarnated back into my life, I said, "Yes, it is my husband."

At the time I was married to Walt. I went home and told him we had a Civil War incarnation together. I asked if I could hypnotize him to see what he would get. Walt was the kind of man who, if he were fabricating something, would pretend I was Scarlett O'Hara and he was saving me from the burning city of Atlanta.

While under hypnosis, he said, "We are brothers. You are abandoning me. You always abandoned me." As you know from an earlier chapter, I abandoned him again when I divorced him. After I ran away to Arizona, he followed me. We tried to put the marriage back together but we couldn't. Eventually, I asked him to leave the house. We divorced, never to speak again. However, sixteen years after our divorce, a thought popped into my head that perhaps one of his parents had died.

I private messaged him on Facebook: "Hey Walt, I wondered if one of your parents has died? And by the way, I want to tell you, while I've got your attention, that I am sorry for my share of the responsibility in the demise of our marriage."

He replied, "No, my parents are still alive. But I heard that your mother died, and I'm sorry. I have thought a great deal about you and the kids over the years. And I too, am very sorry for my share of what happened when we were together."

Six months later, at the age of sixty-four, Walt Kuhlman had a heart attack and died. I was picking up on his death and assuming it was one of his parents. We were soul mates. By our communicating, we acknowledged and forgave each other within our Karmic Pattern in this lifetime. That removes some of our baggage as our souls move forward. Do you see the synchronicity between my past life as a Civil War soldier and my son's past life as a Vietnam soldier? And remember in the beginning when I told you that on my father's side, there were soldiers in the Civil War? Also, Walter was my son McKennan's wrestling coach for most of his life. Hence, we have a thread of energy that goes through the generations and creates patterns in life.

If you cannot find the reasons for some of your challenges by looking at your family origin and your ancestry, then go to a hypnotherapist and have a past life regression so you can figure out all the parts of your Karmic Profile, past and present.

In Their Own Words

> *Back in January or February, Melinda told me I would be contacted by my old employer, Delta Air Lines, in March or April about returning to work. She also indicated she didn't actually see me in my old job until August. My old boss contacted me in late March about bringing me back. He wasn't sure when it would play out but he would keep me posted and he did. The best part is that August 4 is my official start date back at Delta. You must hear this stuff all the time, but I just had to drop a line and say thanks. I look forward to booking another visit sometime this fall. I can't sing Melinda's praises loud enough. TOO COOL...*
>
> *—Scotty*

Act XI

"Men at some time are masters of their fates;
The fault, dear Brutus, is not in our stars,
But in ourselves, that we are underlings."

William Shakespeare

Emotional Maturity

S ome people have heartbreak that others cannot even imagine. They have gone through things that you might think only happen in movies. They have had so many challenges in one lifetime, it amazes me that they're still standing. I have spent time with people who have had experiences that make their lives a tribute to grace and style under pressure. They resonate as an example of faith and dignity and serve as a testament to unwavering love of what is important. It is such an honor for me to be in the presence of these people.

If you could spend one day with me, you would see by the light in their eyes, the miracles that happen for people when they are true to the essence of faith. I absolutely believe this is the goodness of mankind.

I don't even know where to start as there are so many examples of people successfully enduring hardships. I'll begin with someone whom I met many years ago. Her husband killed himself by shooting himself in the head. At first, he was behind her with his hand on her throat and the gun cocked to her temple. But instead, he put the gun to his own temple, pulled the trigger and fell to the ground behind her, bathing her in blood splatter.

Needless to say, this was beyond reason and there is no explanation for his actions. How can you explain crazy? When she came to me, the word devastation hardly would describe her energy. During the session when her husband "came in," it was with the full fury of who he was in life. I had no explanation for it, as I had always believed that once we get to the other side, our egos are left behind.

Nevertheless, I gave her the full spewing of his anger and hurt as he talked to her through me. I had never before and have not since encountered a spirit I would label as "evil," but I would label him that way. It was a very emotional hour for her indeed, and a very difficult reading for me.

Because I give so many readings, often I do not remember their contents. It is sometimes an embarrassment to me that I may have read for somebody and do not remember. I feel badly because it truly is an intimate time to be the middleman between a person and their loved one on the other side. I have come to accept that this is just the "business" part of what I do. I have to remind myself that it does not mean I am not honoring people. But I certainly remember this incident—and will always remember it.

One day I received a note from a lady who had come for a reading a while back. Her note read:

> I don't know if you remember me but I wanted to share with you what has happened since we met. Because of the way he talked to me through you, I knew this was my husband. I had planned on killing myself up until that day. But, when he was done talking to me, during the reading, you shared with me not to give him the power of my energy any longer. It made such sense to me. I knew it was true. So, I wanted you to know that I moved on and that I am happy, remarried, and about to have my first child. Thank you very much.

Well, I thought to myself, that is why he came in the way he did— so she would know it was truly him. Then, she will be able to move on to forgive herself and find the emotional courage to start a new life.

I was teaching a seminar one day and had about 30 people in front of me. I was talking to some people on the other side and a young boy appeared to me. I asked the audience, "Who among you has the child, a teenage boy who is about 13 years old?"

No one answered. The child said to me that he played drums and he had drumsticks in his hand. Again, I asked the audience: "He was the drummer. Who knows this young man?"

Again, no one raised their hand, so I pointed to a woman who I thought was the recipient of this message. "I think he belongs to you," I told her.

She said, "No, my son was in his twenties when he passed away." This woman, who I will call "Susan," had indeed lost her son when he was in his twenties. However, part of her work was to help others with their children crossing.

The next day, a woman, I will call her "Mary," called Susan and said she had just returned from delivering her son's drumsticks to his uncle. "Susan, I heard that you have a support network."

Of course, Susan referred Mary to me because Mary's son had gone out of his way to deliver a message to her. This is the way people from the other side will work to make contact with people on this side.

Both Mary and her husband, I will call "Tom," came to see me. In a spontaneous act of defiance because they would not allow him to date an older girl, their son went upstairs, took his father's service revolver (his father was a policeman at the time), and shot himself to death.

The son, I will call "Jack," deeply regretted hurting his parents this way. Miracles happen all the time in my business, but it was amazing how Jack found a way to get to his parents. Tom and Mary came to talk to Jack several times so they could make some sense out of what happened. Together the three of them, even though Jack was on the other side, worked through all of it. These parents exhibited tremendous emotional courage on this journey and have found a way to live and thrive after the loss of their son.

Tom has since become a Catholic mortician, so he can help other people deal with losses of their own. He turned his Karma into Dharma—meaning that he took the worst of what happened to him and now helps other people get through the same.

He is not the only one who has turned Karma to Dharma. My next couple, I'll call them "Jean" and "Joe," lost their only son, while he was texting and driving, and not wearing a seatbelt. He was late for work and was texting his boss to inform him he was running late. While texting, he lost control of his car and it flipped. The accident was fatal.

His parents came to me only a few short days after he died. As I have previously said, I am booked many months in advance. Someone they knew just happened to have an appointment with me and gave it to them. Their son came in filled with love, light and laughter. He immediately told me his name (I will call him "George") and gave me the numbers on his football jersey.

Within days of his death, his parents had evidence that he was safe and alive. He told us during the reading that someone was standing over him, "annoying him" at the scene. Later, Jean talked to a nurse, a Good Samaritan who had stopped and was on the scene. She told

Jean that someone else had stopped and was praying and chanting over George.

Jean and Joe and I laughed over the fact that indeed that was the annoyance that he described to us. George was always a jokester, the star in his crowd. His parents have gifted sessions with me to many of his friends. Through his death, George has taught many young people that there is life after life.

Still the practical jokester, George has even revealed Christmas presents before they were received. His parents have been working diligently by trying to pass legislation that prohibits texting and driving. They have appeared several times on TV.

I have a client from Texas who also lost a daughter when someone else was driving and texting. The driver went through a stop sign and broadsided the daughter, killing her. These Texas clients are involved also in a campaign to create greater awareness about the dangers of texting and driving.

All three of these families have found the emotional courage to transform their losses into working platforms for preventing others from experiencing similar tragedies. George's father honored his son's passing when he decided to become a policeman so he could dedicate himself to helping other people.

In my last example of emotional courage, I will use the woman's real name, Karen Perry, because she's had a book written about her journey through her grief.

Karen came to me right after her three children, Morgan, age 9; Logan, 8; and Luke, 6; died in a plane crash on the eve of Thanksgiving in 2011, along with their father and two other men. Her journey is chronicled in her book, *Angels Three*.

I remember when I first met Karen; I was embarrassed by what I said to her in the lobby when I came out to meet her and usher her into my office. She was with a friend and they were carrying some of the children's toys as they were told that I did psychometry (holding an object that gave me the energy to connect with the person on the other side).

Because I believe in humor and the fact that laughter raises a vibration that allows for a better contact with the other side, I usually try to make my clients laugh even in the throes of their darkest hours.

I said to them, "Who is coming in with me and who is going to stay here and play with the toys?" They both laughed and came into my office. I was the first medium Karen had ever visited and the kids did a great job of coming through for their mother, letting her know they were safe. She still visits a couple of times a year just to make the "phone call." Recently I was very blessed to have her on my *Angel Show* (an Internet program on my website, MelindaVail.com)

When Elliot, my grandson, was young, he loved to play "restaurant." He would pretend he was the waiter and would take my order. After I placed my order, he would ask me for my name. I thought that was very funny and demonstrated how often my daughter must go to Starbucks.

I would reply that my name is Melinda. He would say, "I've heard about you."

My response was, "Really Elliot—what did you hear about Grandma?"

Without any hesitation, he replied, "Grandma, I heard that you have a very important job."

"Elliot, what does Grandma do?" I asked.

"You know, Grandma!" he said. "You take people in your office that are crying and you make them laugh."

Laughing in the face of adversity is truly a mark of someone who has emotional courage. Emotional courage is a reflection of emotional intelligence and maturity. People with emotional courage find the ability to walk through situations that cause them pain and fear. Once they can do this, they come out on the other side with the ability to help others.

After twenty-three years of being a medium and an intuitive, I could tell you many stories about so many people who have managed to take horrendously shattering situations and turn them into a place where they find the essence of their own spirit. Many people who have suffered great loss in their Karmic Profile have found ways to move through it spiritually and redefine themselves as spiritual beings.

In Their Own Words

I have spoken with Melinda Vail two times and have been totally blown away by my experience with her and the insight that she was able to provide me within my life, the life of loved ones and the life of those who have passed away. I spoke to Melinda in 2014 when she told me that she saw a break across my mom's chest. Melinda told me that my mom should have a breast exam and get this checked out as she may have the early stages of breast cancer. I informed my mom of this and she made an appointment and went to her doctor about a month after my reading. At the appointment, my mom was told that she did in fact have stage 0 breast cancer. The doctor told my mom how lucky she was that they had caught it this early and that she was able to be treated right away. My mom is now breast cancer free and doing well!! Without Melinda's insight, we would never have caught the breast cancer so early. We are eternally grateful to Melinda and her ability to utilize her amazing gift to help others.

—Nicole

Act XII

"Love sought is good, but given unsought, is better."

William Shakespeare

The Law of Attraction

C ontinuing to understand our Karmic Profile means that we have to watch the signs and signals of the Universe. We must learn to understand the Law of Attraction. In previous chapters I have shown you how the Law of Attraction works in relationships through the energetic frequency of that profile in nature and nurture.

The Universe and the Law of Attraction often work in other ways that synchronize information and help you understand who you are and who you are supposed to be. The Universe never stops exchanging information with you and showing you a direction or a signpost to navigate your way through life.

I have a story of synchronicity where the Universe made sure I knew that I was supposed to work with death and dying. I will start the story by telling you that my son-in-law put himself through college by working in mortuary support. That means that he would use his van to transport dead bodies from their current location to the mortuary. His job and school kept him very busy, so he and my daughter had little time to date. Often she would go on a "ride-along" so they could see each other.

One day, I got a phone call from Dr. Elisabeth Kubler-Ross's assistant. She said that Dr. Kubler-Ross had heard about me and wanted me to come to her residence to give her a reading.

Elisabeth was a Swiss-American psychiatrist who wrote about the five stages of grief; she was the author of groundbreaking books on death and dying. Talk about a compliment! To be asked to speak with her? I was beyond flattered.

The assistant instructed me to meet her in the town where Elisabeth lived, which was a considerable distance from my office, and then follow her to Elisabeth's home in the country. When we arrived at the house, the assistant got out of her car and told me, "Don't call her anything but Dr. Ross, and don't touch her." She further directed, "Go through that front door." Then she took off in her car.

I opened the door and spontaneously, without even thinking, called out, "Elisabeth?" I could hear her as she chuckled to herself and called to me, "In here."

I went into her living room and said to her, "I feel like the Pope has just asked me to do Mass." She laughed and held out her hand for me to take it. I gave her a reading and we had a fine afternoon. She asked me to stay for tea and signed several of her books for me. I never saw her again but she wrote to me once or twice. I know this was my sign to continue my work.

Years later, my daughter was on a ride-along mortuary transport with her future husband, and she called me late at night. My children know better than to call me at night as I go to bed very early and a late-night call always freaks me out.

I answered the phone with the panic voice, "What's the matter, honey?"

She exclaimed, "Mama, Elisabeth Kubler-Ross has died!"

"How do you know that?" I asked.

Excitedly, she replied, "Because, Mama, we have her in the van!"

I can't imagine what my Karma was with this very unique and special woman, but I know there must be some type of connection between us because of the way the Universe put it all in order for me. My take on it was that the afternoon we spent together was just as special for her as it was for me. Her soul wanted me to be one of the first ones to know that she had gone to the other side. It was an amazing orchestration of Universal energy.

Many times the Universe will speak and show a direction. You just have to be open to it and learn how to recognize it as it may not be as blatant as my connection with Elisabeth. It is how you handle and honor these directions that make the differences in your life.

Remember, whenever you are in ego, you are not in a place to be in honor of yourself. The ego is frail and inhumane; it takes us into places where only our shadow resides. Our spirit is filled with light and is in partnership with the Universe. It takes us into places where we understand our shadow and no longer identify with it. That is what puts us in a place to understand our Karmic Profile. It allows us to move into neutral energy and be present for our self.

Another time the Law of Attraction showed me my connection to my mediumship and connection to Spirit was when I was doing a seminar with James Van Praagh. We were doing a "Night of Spirit," which is a stage performance where we do readings together in front of hundreds of people.

James asked me to go first. My second connection that night was with a priest who showed himself in his Cassock. He gave me his name and some family background. A woman stood up in the audience and claimed him. She said, "He is my cousin; you all know him. He is Pope John Paul II."

I knew this woman; I had done readings for her and the Pope had come to speak to her before. This time, however, he gave his real name and his family background. To confirm this, after the event, I looked up information about him. He channeled to the crowd and his message was that we were on the cusp of having this world end if we did not start being collaborative and connecting to each other with love, respect, and harmony.

James Van Praagh looked at me with incredulity and queried, "You are channeling the Pope?"

I said, "I guess I am."

This was full circle energy from the time I was a little girl, when the priest came out on the altar and revealed to me that Spirit was honoring my prayers and me. It was another miracle presented to me in my life.

In Their Own Words

Dear Melinda,

I hope you are well, my friend. I have another lovely story of validation for you! And I always say, you never need validation for your gift from me, because you know how much I believe in you, but this I had to share.

This past March at Barnes & Noble, I was there with my dear friend Heather. You told me, through Spirit of course, that TJ was around his new brother-in-law and that he really loved him. You also shared that Sheena and Jeff would move this year. Once they moved, you explained, they would get pregnant, and that TJ was with this baby getting the baby ready for our family. At that time, Sheena had just told me they were not going to move, but would be signing their lease for one more year. BUT, they were still planning to try to get pregnant. So, I was open to the move part, knowing that something could change, and that Spirit told you that for a reason. Of course, I was ecstatic about all of it!

In June, Sheena and Jeff changed their mind, and began looking for houses. They found what they loved and moved into their brand new beautiful home in July. Also, they had been trying to get pregnant since March, but no luck by mid-summer. They finished their move in August and traveled to the beach with Tim, Paddy and me.

THEN, in mid-September, they announced to just Tim and me and Pat that they are five weeks pregnant, and the baby is due May ninth! It's no coincidence that TJ's birthday is May tenth. Everything you predicted came true! At this point, we were sworn to secrecy by Sheena and Jeff, as they wanted to wait to tell other family members and friends.

And this is where it gets really good! Three days after Sheena and Jeff announced to us the good news, my nephew sent me a text message. In it he told me that he had just had a session with you, and that he had some good news for us. He said, "Not only is TJ doing really well, but he is also very proud of his sister, and congratulations to her pregnancy and baby in 2016!" WOW! I really loved this. And first thing I said to Tim is, "Oh, I can picture TJ with his impish grin, as he tells family members before we can! Ha!" Too funny!

Now that they have officially announced it, I can tell you. We are so excited about this amazing time in our lives! Thank you for all of the support for our family... our lives are enriched by you.

Much love and many Blessings.

—Justine

Epilogue

"To be, or not to be: that is the question."

William Shakespeare

Remember, your Karmic Profile includes your soul purpose, soul contract, soul learning, process, and the opportunity to work through it on the earth plane.

As you saw from my personal profile, your Karmic agreement is not something you can escape. The only time it "traps" you, however, is when it holds you hostage. I have worked in the psychic/medium field for 25 years and I'm good at it—yet I still have to work out my personal Karmic debts.

If you are not learning and growing on this planet, then you are dead. If anyone ever tells you they are so "enlightened" they have nothing left to work on, then they are either foolish or in ego. Run. This existence doesn't work that way.

Imagine that you are a giant switchboard and "plug in" all attributes of yourself to find your spiritual identity. You can start by looking at your ancestors. Find out what you can.

First, look at energy patterns. If you are adopted, your soul chose both backgrounds, biological and adopted. You may find similarities between both.

Next, look at the energy of your upbringing, the placement in your family, and the relationships between you and your parents and siblings. How did your parents interact with each other? What influences did you have in your youth? Perhaps you received messages from teachers or mentors. Were there any moves, injuries, or traumas? Find the subtle energy of what was placed in your subconscious mind. There is importance in the language and words, the tones and attitudes that created you.

Third, meditate or pray about past lives. A helpful way to find out about past lives is to look at past *déjà vu*. Write about your impression of your past life. Another way is to focus on what resonates in a work of art, a period of time, a country, or a historical event. Try creating timelines. Look at old photos and see when you were happy, sad, angry or afraid. Look at your eyes. Then shift focus to your adult life. Find patterns of energy in relationships. See if you are working out the energy of your mother, the energy of your father, or both.

Plug all of this into the switchboard to see who you really are, what you believe about yourself, what makes you tick.

When you figure out who you are, find the emotional courage and maturity to own it. Be honest about it. Be responsible for it. Laugh about it. Mourn it. Talk about it and set yourself free.

The Universe will then talk to you with synchronicity and direction. You will always be shown direction and given guidance. The ego will be satisfied and the soul will be gratified. You will own your Karmic Profile. It will not own you.

Namaste,

Melinda

Acknowledgments

I would like to acknowledge my beloved husband, William, for his support and faith in this book; my son, Izzy, for all his hard work; and my dear friend, Duffy McMahon, who sharpened her pen and edited this work for me.

About Melinda Vail

A s an intuitive therapist, medium, author, lecturer and certi-fied hypnotherapist, Melinda has a very successful practice in Tempe, Arizona. Countless people have benefited from Melinda's counseling and intuitive work. She has appeared on both local and national television and radio shows.

Melinda is also an accomplished speaker at the national level and gives workshops across the country to promote spiritual growth. Her work with police agencies helping to solve cold cases and donating her time to provide grief counseling through her suicide survivor and other related workshops has garnered her the nickname, "The Medium Who Makes a Difference."

Melinda's website is www.melindavail.com.

Edgor Casey
4-18-21

CPSIA information can be obtained
at www.ICGtesting.com
Printed in the USA
FFOW05n1521191017

9 780999 215760